Famous & Fun Rock

9 Appealing Piano Arrangements

Carol Matz

D1278513

Famous & Fun Rock, Book 3, contains 9 carefully selected popular rock hits. Each piece has been arranged especially for elementary to late elementary pianists, yet remains faithful to the sound of the original. The arrangements can be used as a supplement to any method. Simple eighth-note rhythms are used, but dotted-quarter notes are avoided. The selections are arranged with no more than one sharp or flat in the key signature. The optional duet parts for teacher or parent add to the fun!

Carol Matz

Produced by
Alfred Music Publishing Co., Inc.
P.O. Box 10003
Van Nuys, CA 91410-0003
alfred.com

ISBN-10: 0-7390-9605-2
ISBN-13: 978-0-7390-9605-5

Blue Moon

Music by Richard Rodgers
Lyrics by Lorenz Hart
Arranged by Carol Matz

Moderately fast

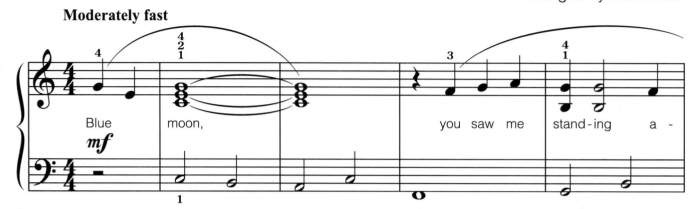

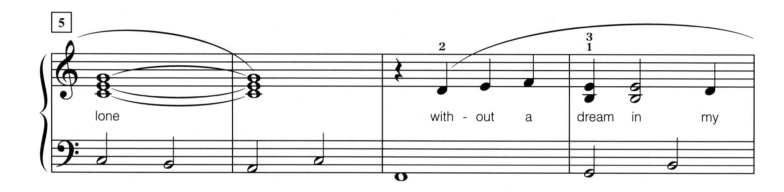

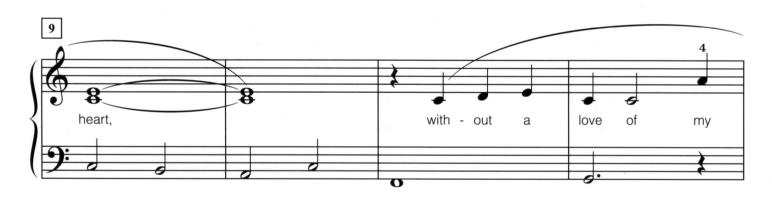

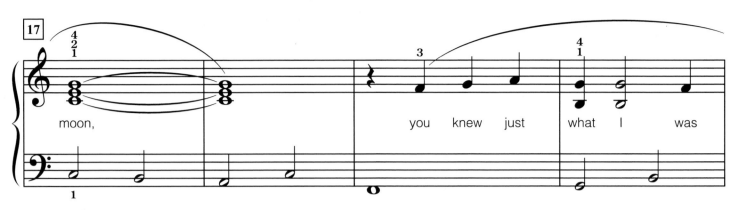

moon,

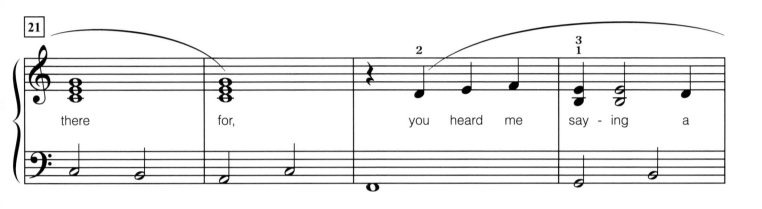

you knew just what I was

there for,

you heard me say - ing a

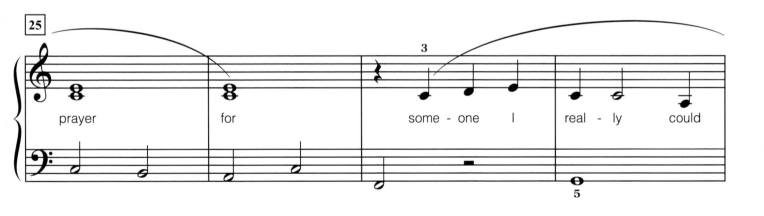

prayer for

some - one I real - ly could

care for.

rit.

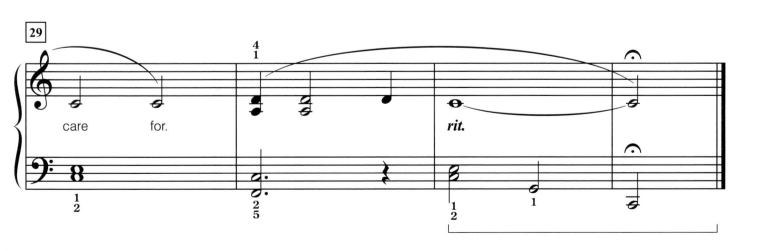

The Lion Sleeps Tonight

New Lyric and Revised Music by
George David Weiss, Hugo Peretti
and Luigi Creatore
Arranged by Carol Matz

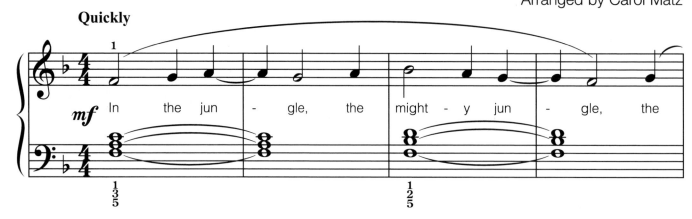

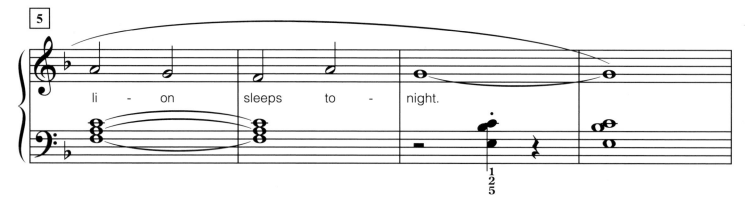

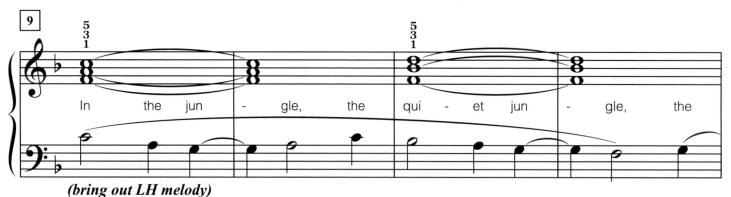

(bring out LH melody)

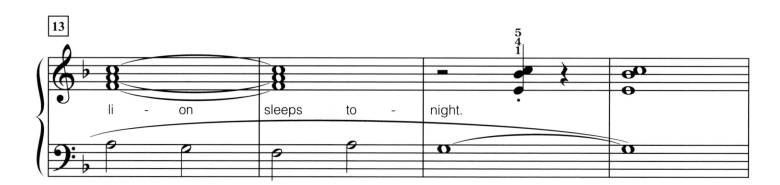

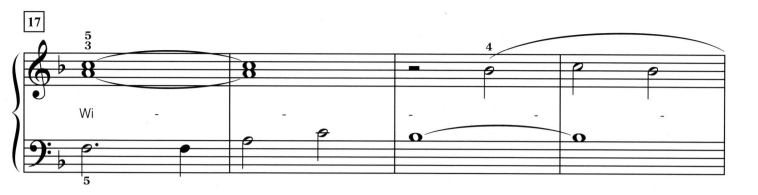

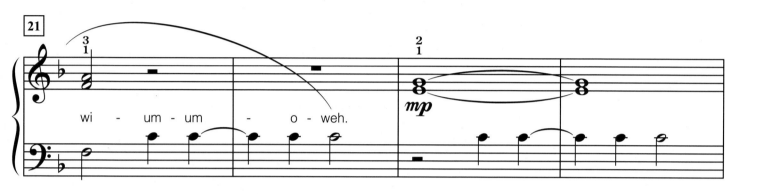

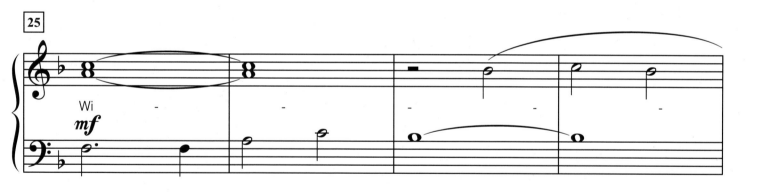

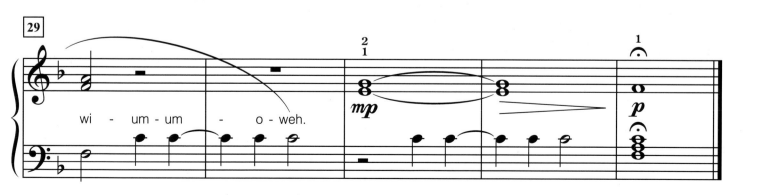

Killing Me Softly

Words and Music by
Charles Fox and Norman Gimbel
Arranged by Carol Matz

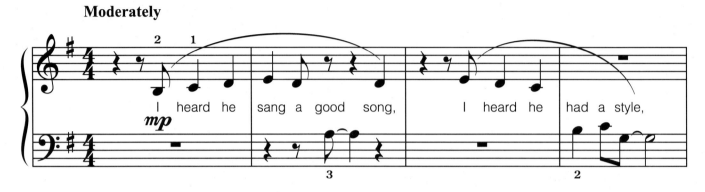

I heard he sang a good song,   I heard he   had a style,

DUET PART (Student plays one octave higher)

7

Breakaway

Words and Music by Matthew Gerrard,
Bridget Benenate and Avril Lavigne
Arranged by Carol Matz

Quickly

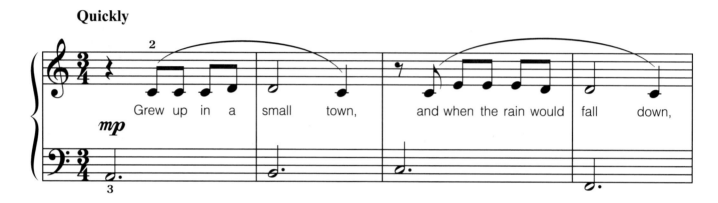

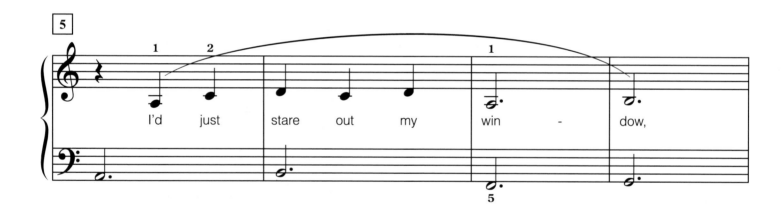

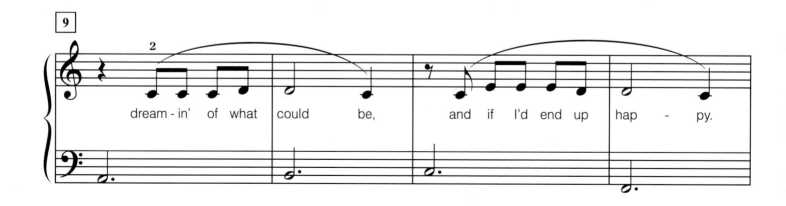

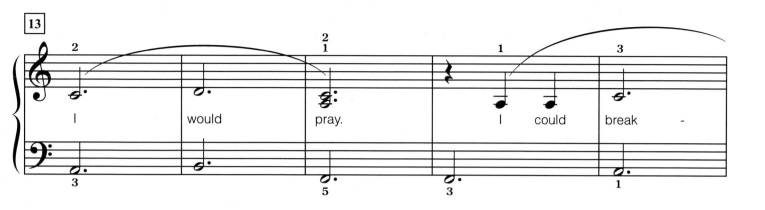

I would pray. I could break -

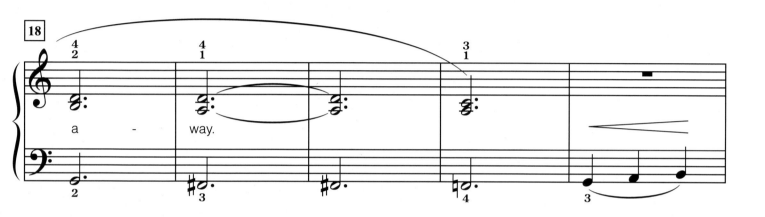

a - way.

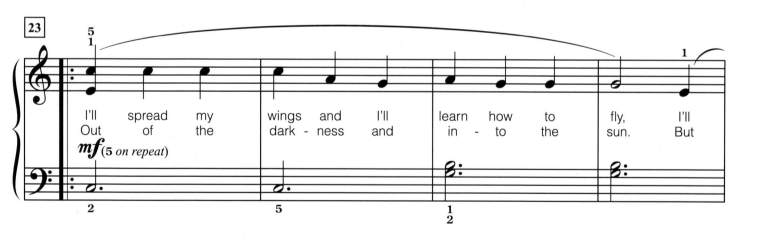

I'll spread my wings and I'll learn how to fly, I'll
Out of my the dark - ness and in - to the sun. But

mf (**5** *on repeat*)

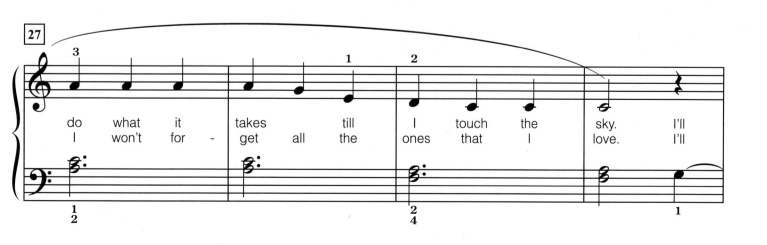

do what it takes till I touch the sky. I'll
I won't for - get all the ones that I love. I'll

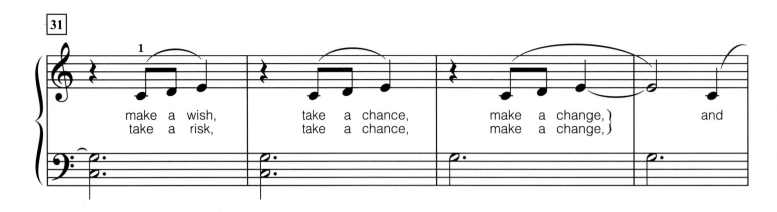

make a wish,
take a risk,

take a chance,
take a chance,

make a change,
make a change,

and

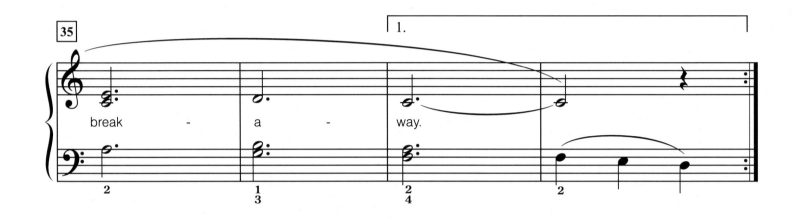

break - a - way.

1.

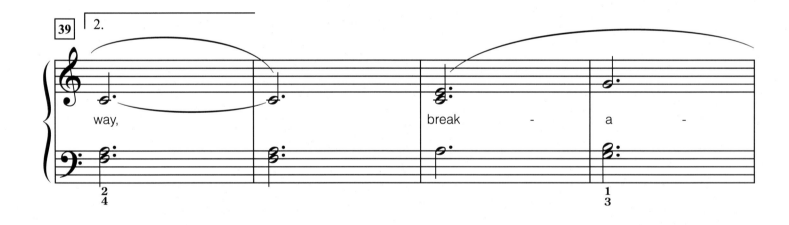

2.

way,

break - a -

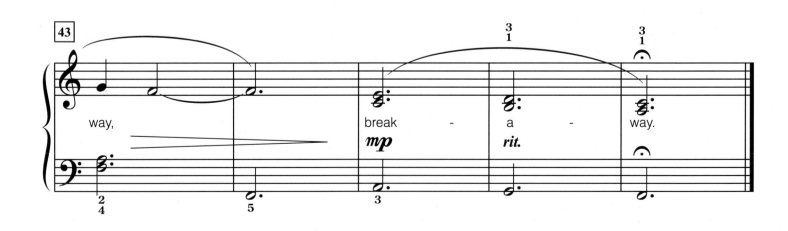

way,

break - a - way.

mp

rit.

You're the One That I Want

Words and Music by John Farrar
Arranged by Carol Matz

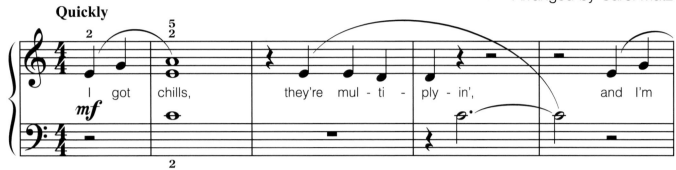

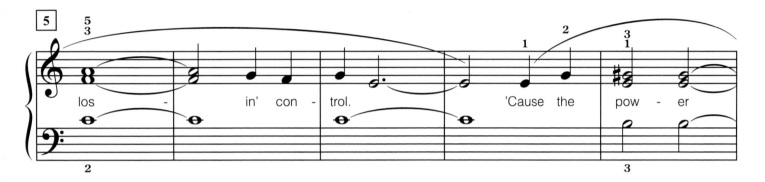

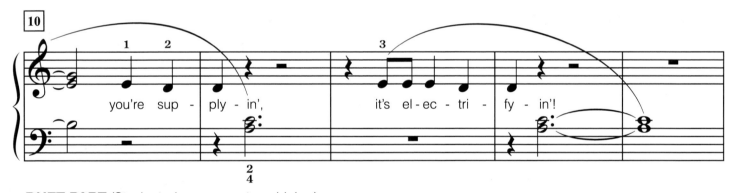

DUET PART (Student plays one octave higher)

You bet-ter shape up, 'cause I need a man

and my heart is set on you.

Play 3 times

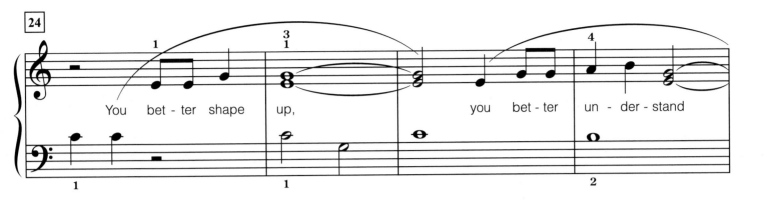

You bet - ter shape up, you bet - ter un - der - stand

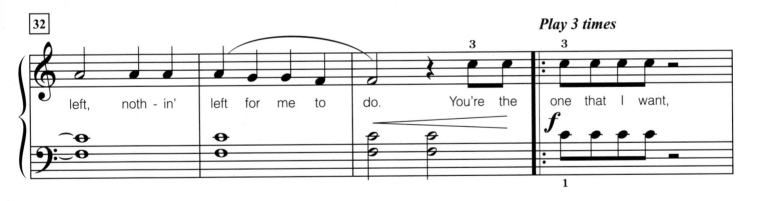

to my heart I must be true. Noth - in'

Play 3 times

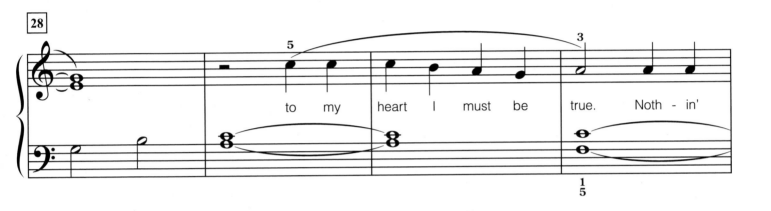

left, noth - in' left for me to do. You're the one that I want,

f

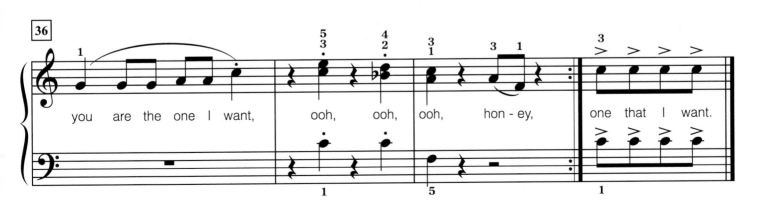

you are the one I want, ooh, ooh, ooh, hon - ey, one that I want.

Gotta Be Somebody

Lyrics by Chad Kroeger
Music by Nickelback
Arranged by Carol Matz

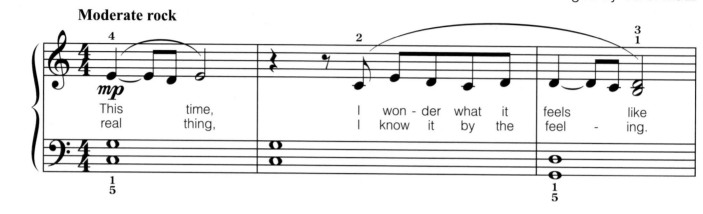

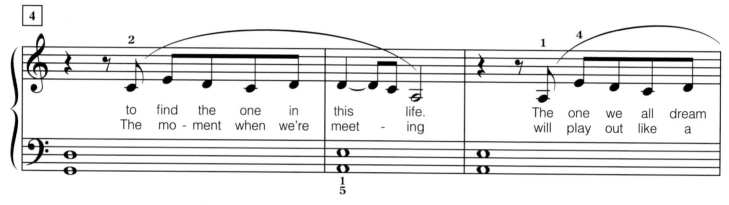

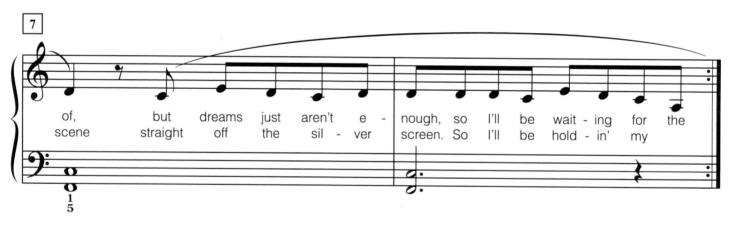

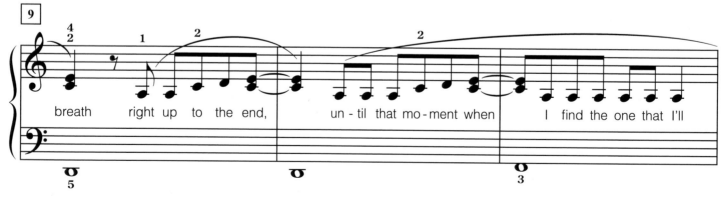

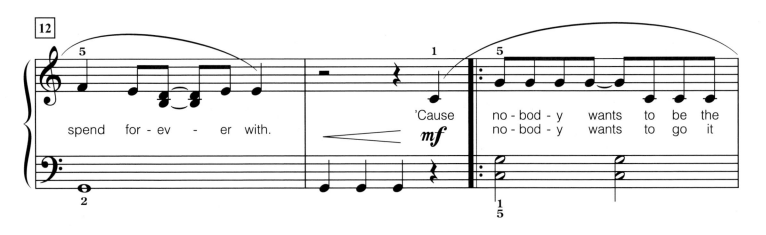

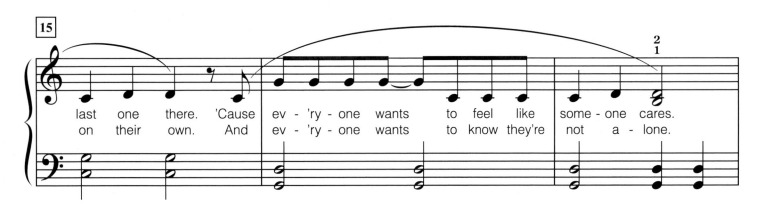

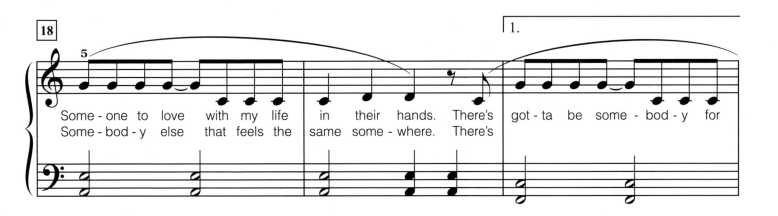

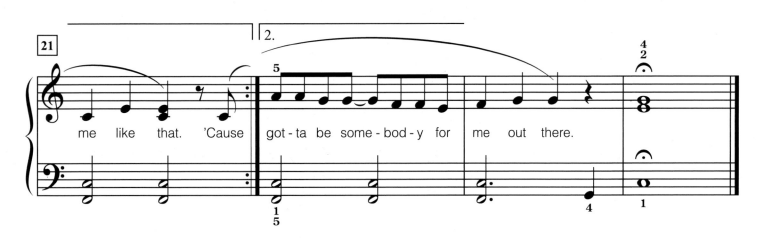

Wake Me Up When September Ends

Words by Billie Joe
Music by Green Day
Arranged by Carol Matz

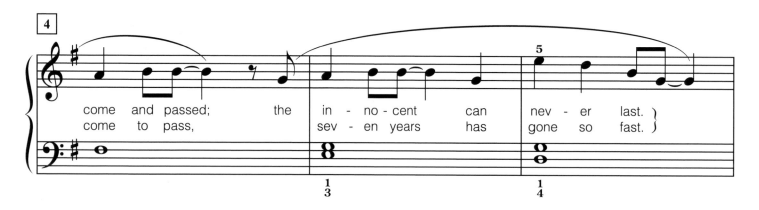

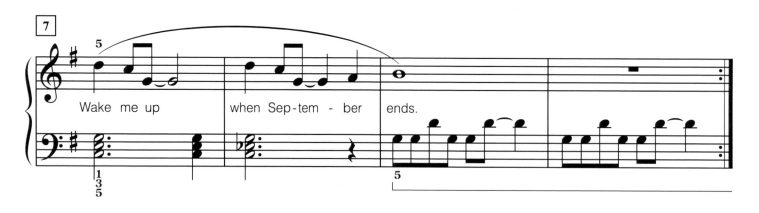

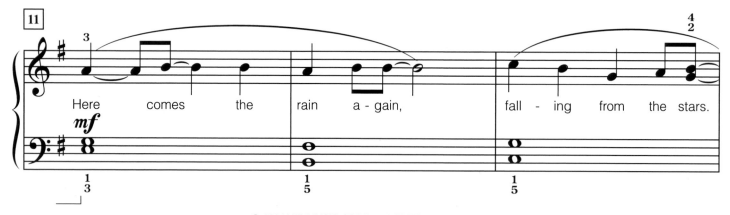

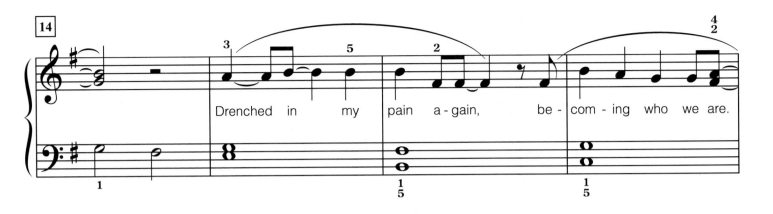

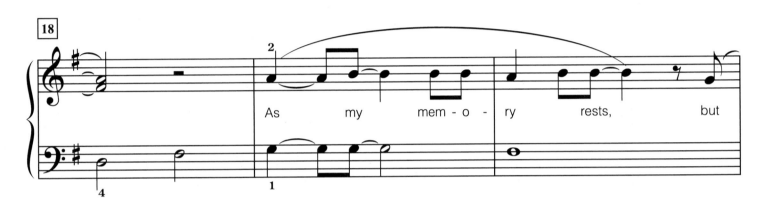

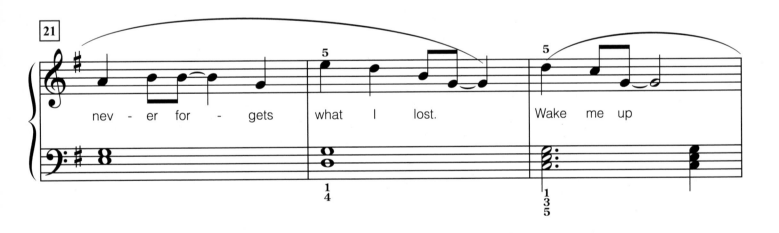

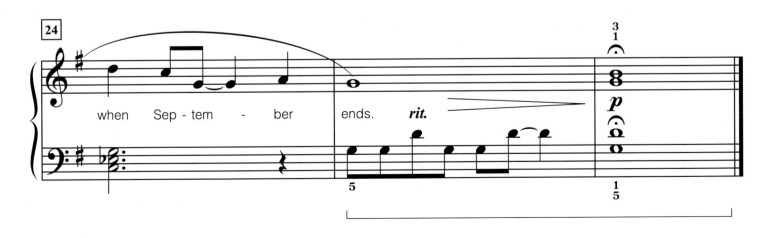

Don't Stop Believin'

Words and Music by Jonathan Cain,
Neal Schon and Steve Perry
Arranged by Carol Matz

Moderately

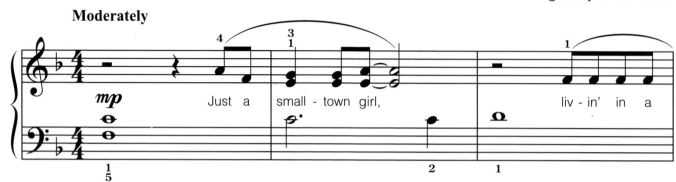

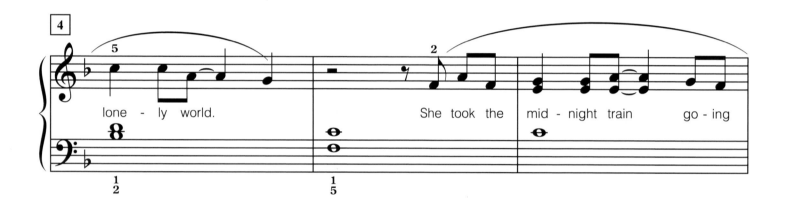

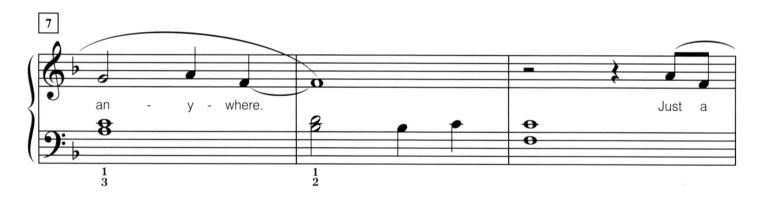

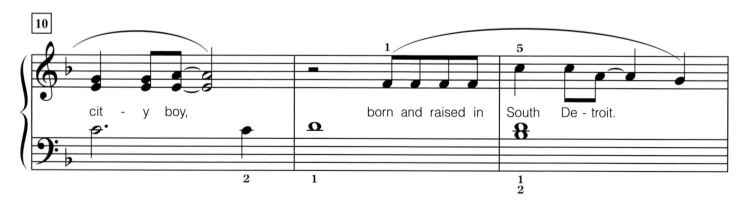

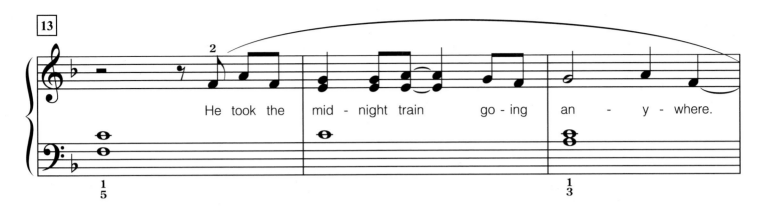

He took the mid - night train go - ing an - y - where.

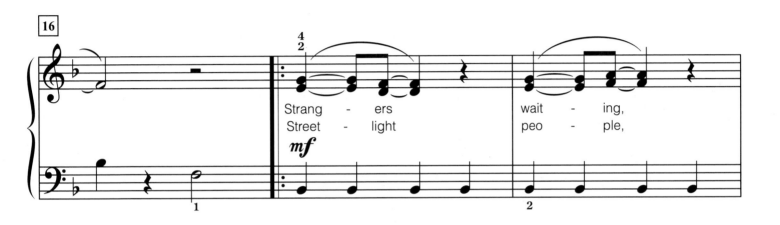

Strang - ers wait - ing,
Street - light peo - ple,

mf

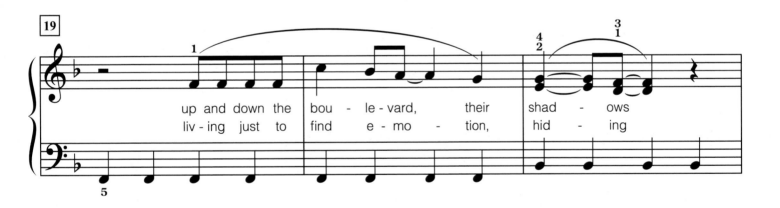

up and down the bou - le - vard, their shad - ows
liv - ing just to find e - mo - tion, hid - ing

1.

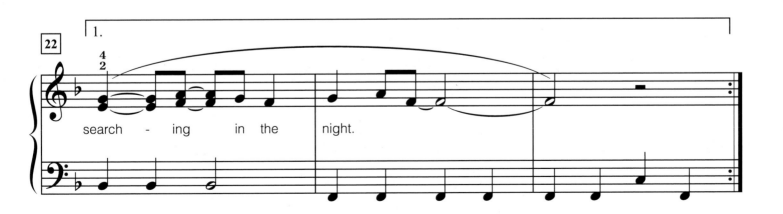

search - ing in the night.

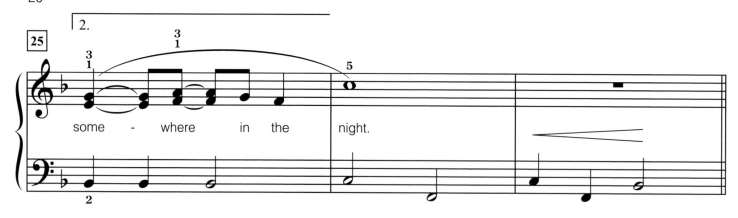

some - where in the night.

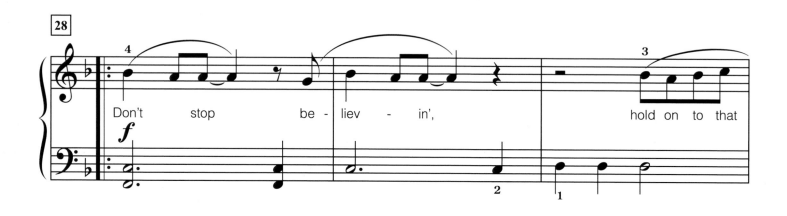

Don't stop be - liev - in', hold on to that

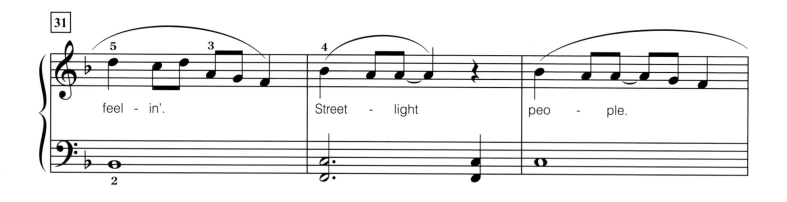

feel - in'. Street - light peo - ple.

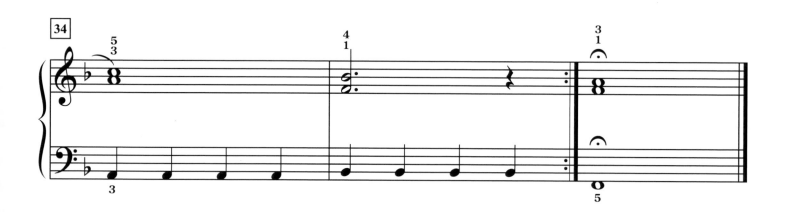

Rock and Roll

Words and Music by Jimmy Page, Robert Plant,
John Paul Jones and John Bonham
Arranged by Carol Matz

DUET PART (Student plays one octave higher)

23